BLAIRSVILLE SENIOR HIGH SCHOOL
BLAIRSVILLE, PENNA

International Organizations

The United Way

Rennay Craats

WEIGL PUBLISHERS INC.

Published by Weigl Publishers Inc.
123 South Broad Street, Box 227
Mankato, MN 56002
USA

Web site: www.weigl.com

Library of Congress Cataloging-in-Publication Data

Craats, Rennay.
  United Way / Rennay Craats.
      p. cm. -- (International organizations)
Summary: Highlights the history, membership, mission, goals, and
achievements of the United Way of America and other United Way
organizations elsewhere in the world. Includes human interest stories, maps,
timelines, Web sites, and suggestions for further reading.
Includes bibliographical references and index.
  ISBN 1-59036-022-2 (lib. bdg. : alk. paper)
 1. United Way of America--Juvenile literature. 2. United
Way--Juvenile literature. 3. Charities--Juvenile literature. 4.
Charities--United States--Juvenile literature. [1. United Way of
America. 2. United Way. 3. Charities.] I. Title. II. Series.
  HV97.U553 C73 2002
  361.8--dc21

                                              2002006564

Printed in Canada
1 2 3 4 5 6 7 8 9 0   06 05 04 03 02

Credits

Project Coordinator
Michael Lowry
Copy Editor
Jennifer Nault
Photo Researcher
Gayle Murdoff
Design and Layout
Warren Clark
Bryan Pezzi

Photo Credits

Every reasonable effort has been made to trace ownership and to obtain
permission to reprint copyright material. The publishers would be pleased to
have any errors or omissions brought to their attention so that they may be
corrected in subsequent printings.

Cover: PhotoDisc/Getty Images; **Corbis Corporation:** pages 10, 26; **CORBIS/MAGMA:** page
21; **Corel Corporation:** page 4; **Howard Davies/Exile Images:** pages 13, 19, 23 top; **Digital
Vision Ltd.:** page 22; **Jeff Greenberg/MaXx Images:** page 3; **Matthew McDermott/ Corbis
Sygma/MAGMA:** page 25; **Michigan United Way:** page 27; **National Archives of Canada/PA-
168131:** page 20; **Reuters NewMedia Inc./CORBIS/MAGMA:** page 7; **Skjold Photographs:**
pages 5, 9, 11, 12, 15; **United Way of America:** pages 18, 23 bottom.

Text Credits

Reuters: quotation on page 24.

Contents

What is the United Way?

The United Way of America (UWA) is a non-profit organization dedicated to helping communities across the United States. The United Way movement is made up of 1,400 independent United Way organizations. Together, the volunteers in these organizations work hard to improve the lives of citizens and bring communities together. The UWA also helps train and support the staff and the large numbers of volunteers that work in community-based projects.

The UWA provides services to support families, build safe neighborhoods, and help people without food or shelter or people facing physical or emotional challenges. Each member organization helps the people and communities in its region. All of the money raised by or donated to a member organization stays in that area. It is spent on projects to help local people. Over the years, the United Way of America has helped raise billions of dollars to assist millions of people.

> **"It's about making a measurable difference ... Our unique approach to community building starts by identifying the most urgent issues in communities."**
>
> **Dimon McFerson, UWA**

The United Way provides funding for non-profit organizations, such as Habitat for Humanity. Habitat for Humanity builds simple, affordable housing for those in need.

Each year, the United Way provides about 1.7 billion dollars for youth-related programs such as after-school tutoring programs.

Quick Fact ·······················

United Way organizations in other countries usually have different names. Some are known as Matan, Fondo Unido, or Dividendo, depending on where they are and what language is spoken in the area.

Just the Facts

Founded: The first United Way organization was started in 1887. It was called Charity Organizations Society. The term "United Way" was not used until the 1970s.

Founder: Henry Ford II called a meeting to launch the United Health and **Welfare** Fund on July 15, 1947. He introduced a new style of fund-raising.

Mission: The UWA works to improve people's lives through local community programs.

Number of member organizations: There are approximately 1,400 United Way organizations in the U.S. There are United Way organizations in forty-one other countries worldwide.

Scope of Work: The UWA helps raise money for programs and services to improve people's lives. These programs include health care, rebuilding after disasters and other emergencies, providing education and training, and providing development programs for children.

An Organization is Born

The idea for the United Way in the United States began in 1887 in Denver, Colorado. With so many families moving west at that time, more money was needed to support and help people. In 1888, the first campaign was launched. It raised $21,700 for people in need.

In 1947, Henry Ford II helped launch the United Health and Welfare Fund of the State of Michigan. The United Fund aimed to reduce the competition between charities for donations. It also brought people together from many different organizations. It took some time before all the agencies could agree to work together.

During the first United Fund campaign in Michigan in early 1949, many important agencies, such as the Heart Association, did not participate. Eventually, they learned to accept this new method of fund-raising. By the end of 1949, this new fund-raising process was running smoothly. For instance, the United Foundation Torch Drive of Detroit raised more than $9 million. It also set the stage for decades of charity and goodwill to come.

> "But whether [people] live on the plains or in the valleys, whether they live in slums or isolated villages ... they have one thing in common: they do not want charity. They want a chance."
>
> **James D. Wolfensohn, President of the World Bank Group**

Quick Fact •

The United Way organizations in the United States contribute to more than 45,000 local agencies that help meet the needs of Americans.

PROFILE

United Way's Longtime Supporter

Brian A. Gallagher knows the importance of lending a hand to people in need. When he was growing up, private and public organizations helped his family pay the bills during difficult times. This made him want to help others, too. Brian was born in Chicago and grew up in Indiana. He studied for a degree in social work and a master's degree in business. He was selected by the UWA as a trainee.

For twenty years, Brian has worked at United Way organizations across the U.S. Then, at the beginning of 2002, Brian became the chief executive officer of the United Way of America. He uses his long experience at the United Way to help him run the United Way of America. He took over the organization at a challenging time. A slowing economy and more competition for donation dollars meant it was increasingly difficult for the United Way to maintain its programs. Brian remains confident that the organization can change and grow with the times. By bringing communities and organizations together, Brian is sure that the UWA will continue to provide programs and services that make the United States a better place to live.

> **"We're not a fund-raising organization, we're a community impact organization."**
> **Brian A. Gallagher, CEO of the United Way of America**

The Mission

United Way organizations focus on supporting the people who need them most. The needs vary from community to community. Since each United Way chapter is independent, it makes its own decisions about where to target its programs. The chapters work in partnership with local schools, businesses, neighborhood associations, and churches to provide services to people in need. These services include meal programs, youth programs, health insurance, and affordable housing.

Although many chapters share the same goals, each United Way organization has its own board members who are volunteers. Each chapter also has its own budget and donation targets. Some United Way organizations raise millions of dollars every year. Others raise only a few thousand dollars. Despite differences in size, every United Way organization in the U.S. works toward making local communities more caring.

> "Success is not how much money you raise, it's whether you can actually measurably move the needle on impacting people's lives."
>
> Brian A. Gallagher, CEO of UWA

Quick Fact

During the 2000–2001 United Way campaigns, the organization collected a record $4.7 billion. The Chicago branch raised the most money, at $96.2 million. United Way of New York came in second with $93.6 million raised.

Many of the people in the United States who visit food banks are employed, but they do not earn enough money to adequately feed their families. The United Way regularly funds food programs to help feed low-income families.

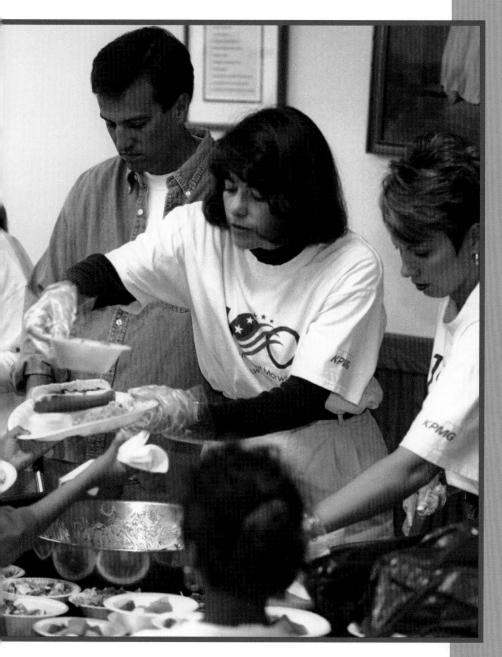

The United Way of America:

- is the second-largest provider of health and human services in the country. It is second only to the U.S. federal government.

- is the training center for the entire United Way organization. It helps chapters as well as businesses involved in United Way campaigns better serve the communities in which they fund-raise.

- contributes to new and changing policies. The UWA works with congress to create programs that will ease problems in American communities.

- relies heavily on volunteers. More than 3 million volunteers across the country help make the United Way movement a success.

- is headquartered in Alexandria, Virginia.

- helps establish programs at workplaces across the country for employee donations.

Key Issues

Disaster Relief

While the UWA cannot prevent disasters, it can certainly lend a hand after one has occurred. United Way chapters throughout the country are ready to help if disasters strike. These can be natural disasters, such as earthquakes or hurricanes, or human-made disasters, such as explosions. United Way chapters work with the agencies already in place in the affected areas.

> "What do we live for ... if not to make life less difficult for each other?"
>
> **Marilyn Cavazos, United Way Community Services**

By **collaborating** with such organizations as the American Red Cross and the Salvation Army, the UWA is able to deliver aid more quickly and efficiently.

The United Way draws on its enormous team of volunteers and contacts to help in a crisis. The United Way organizations are available immediately after a disaster and they continue to help for as long as they are needed. Beyond tending to the needs of the victims, the UWA also helps heal the community and plan for the future.

The United Way works to provide aid to victims of natural disasters, such as earthquakes, floods, and hurricanes.

CASE STUDY
Hurricane Floyd

In 1999, a powerful storm hit the United States. Hurricane Floyd caused millions of people to leave their homes along the east coast to find a safer place inland. Hurricane Floyd caused more than $3 billion worth of damage in North Carolina and New Jersey, mostly due to flooding. Forty people were killed.

United Way volunteers provided support to people whose homes and businesses had been damaged. United Ways from around the country donated $166,550 to help the relief effort. Some branches also sent staff to help rebuild the communities. Volunteers filled sandbags to protect homes from floodwaters. Richard Croskery, president of the United Way of Pit County, promised that the United Way would remain long after the crisis had left the front pages of the newspapers and the National Guard had gone home. It is that same spirit of determination that has given victims hope after an unimaginable disaster such as Hurricane Floyd.

"Our job is to be there until the **salvage**, restoration, and rebuilding is completed. And our job is to remain here, where we've been for the last forty years, ready to assist in the next crisis, large or small."
Richard Croskery,
United Way of Pit County

Keeping People Healthy

The UWA is part of the National Board. This is a group of six volunteer agencies. The National Board gives **grants** to agencies that assist areas in desperate need of help. These grants go to programs that provide food banks and soup kitchens, shelters, and financial assistance. In 1997, more than 85 million meals were distributed, more than 10,500 organizations were given grants for emergency services, and more than 180,400 utility bills were paid for families in financial trouble.

The United Way of America is also involved in health-care programs. These programs exist to provide people with access to medical treatment or health insurance. The UWA has created "211" to make receiving health services easier. This simple telephone number connects people to the local community-based organizations and government agencies that can help them meet their health needs. Human and health services become easier to find and use, so fewer people go without.

Some United Way chapters have helped people without health insurance. One such program, the Operations Council for Project Access, in Wichita, Kansas, provides medical treatment for those without insurance. Many medical providers joined the effort to supply medication to people who cannot afford it. Similar programs have been introduced by United Way chapters elsewhere in the country.

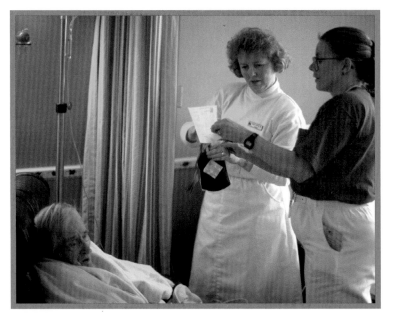

Approximately 47 percent of Americans living below the poverty line do not have health insurance.

CASE STUDY
ProPoor

The United Way International and the United Way organizations of India and Singapore came together to create ProPoor. This nonprofit organization focuses on issues such as poverty, child labor, health, human rights, education, and democracy. Through this organization, people such as 7-year-old Bindu Silwal from Jhapa can obtain help. Bindu has a disease called thalassemia. This means that her body no longer creates new blood. Her life depends on receiving **blood transfusions** each month. To cure this disease, she needs a bone marrow transplant. However, Bindu's family is poor. The operation is expensive, and she would have to travel to another country for treatment. Bindu's family has already spent all of their money on blood transfusions. Without help, Bindu will die. ProPoor has listened to Bindu's cry for help. The organization has an "Appeals" section on its Web site. By visiting www.propoor.com, you can read about people in need like Bindu and find out how to help. Visitors to the Web site can donate money to help some of the people in need.

"It's our bad luck that we cannot help our dying child … If anybody helps me financially, I can take my child to a big hospital."
Krishna Prasad Silwal,
Bindu's Father

Caring for America's Youth

The future lies in the hands of today's children. For that reason, youth development is an important **initiative** for the United Way. There are millions of young people in need in the United States. To help these children, United Way chapters have introduced programs to improve children's lives and the lives of their families. The UWA supports programs dedicated to providing children with the education and other resources they need. UWA considers all factors that add to a child's success, including health, self-esteem, and financial support.

> **"Positive youth development ... is not just about preventing bad things from happening, but giving a nudge to help good things happen."**
>
> **Senator James Jeffords**

The programs funded or sponsored by UWA have many different focuses. Some programs teach children and adults to read. Others work to get youth involved in their communities and to make their city or neighborhoods better places to live. Other programs provide early childhood education. These programs include Success By 6, which deals with children up to the age of 6 in 330 communities across the country. The program Young America Cares! encourages children to join youth groups and participate in training and leadership initiatives. With communities and UWA organizations working together, young people in the United States are being provided with the resources they need for a bright future.

Quick Fact • • • • • • • • • • • • • • • • • •

More than 2 million volunteers work for the United Way International. They help raise more than $723 million every year.

CASE STUDY
Younger Americans Act

The United Way of America has long been involved with children's issues. The UWA has led youth service organizations in the United States to encourage Congress to introduce national policies that protect children. The UWA joined forces with such organizations as Boys & Girls Clubs of America, Save the Children, Alliance for Children and Families, and the YMCA and YWCA, to create the Younger Americans Act (YAA). This piece of **legislation** is the first national policy for young people in the United States. It unites community organizations, agencies, schools, businesses, religious institutions, parents, and children to serve and support youth. The YAA states that youth must have access to five resources. These resources are:

- relationships with caring adults
- safe places that have appropriate activities in which youth can participate
- services that ensure healthy lifestyles
- opportunities to learn useful skills

- opportunities for community service

The YAA was created to prepare young people to become responsible adults in the community. To meet this aim, communities are expected to provide services such as mentoring programs and after-school programs. The YAA legislation plans to provide $5.75 billion over a five-year period to fund youth development across the United States. With more than 80 million children in the country, the YAA is an important national policy.

Around the World

The United Way International is a successful organization due to its strength in numbers. There are many United Way chapters working together to help people around the world. Today, there are United Way organizations in about forty countries including the United States.

Countries with United Way organizations are colored yellow on this map.

CANADA
United Way
of Canada/
Centraide Canada

MEXICO
Fondo Unido I.A.P

GUATEMALA
Fondo Unido
de Guatemala

NICARAGUA
Asociación
Nicaraguense
Americana

COSTA RICA
Asociación de
Empresarios para
el Desarrollo

ECUADOR
Fundación Esquel

COLOMBIA
Fundación Dividendo
por Colombia

JAMAICA
United Way of Jamaica

PUERTO RICO
Fondos Unidos
de Puerto Rico

U.S. VIRGIN ISLANDS
United Way of St. Croix
United Way of
St. Thomas
& St. John

BRAZIL
Associação
Caminhando
Juntos

VENEZUELA
Dividendo
Voluntario Para
La Comunidad

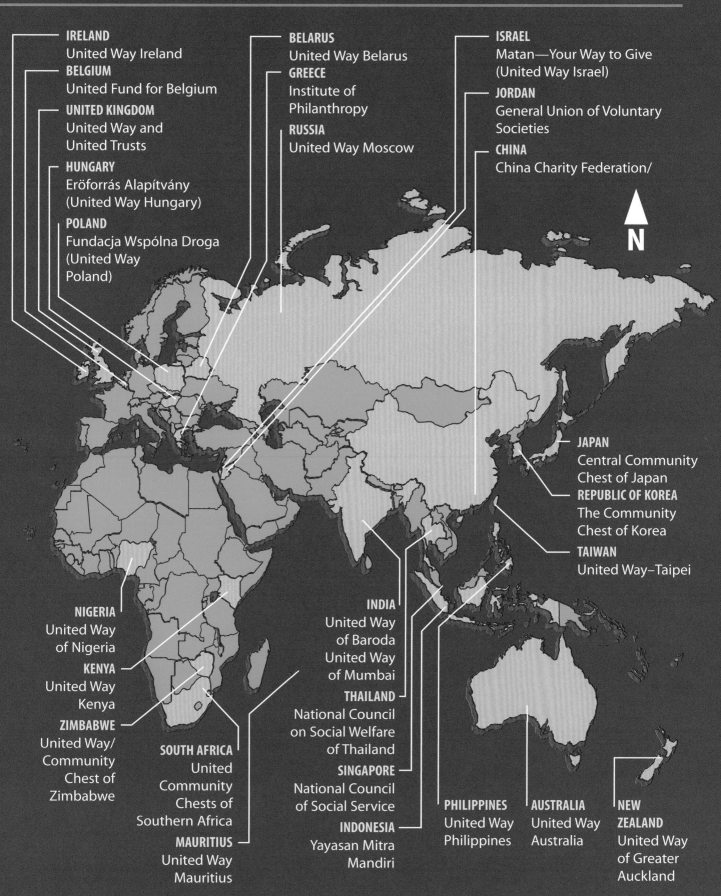

IRELAND
United Way Ireland

BELGIUM
United Fund for Belgium

UNITED KINGDOM
United Way and
United Trusts

HUNGARY
Eröforrás Alapítvány
(United Way Hungary)

POLAND
Fundacja Wspólna Droga
(United Way
Poland)

BELARUS
United Way Belarus

GREECE
Institute of
Philanthropy

RUSSIA
United Way Moscow

ISRAEL
Matan—Your Way to Give
(United Way Israel)

JORDAN
General Union of Voluntary
Societies

CHINA
China Charity Federation/

N

JAPAN
Central Community
Chest of Japan

REPUBLIC OF KOREA
The Community
Chest of Korea

TAIWAN
United Way–Taipei

NIGERIA
United Way
of Nigeria

KENYA
United Way
Kenya

ZIMBABWE
United Way/
Community
Chest of
Zimbabwe

SOUTH AFRICA
United
Community
Chests of
Southern Africa

MAURITIUS
United Way
Mauritius

INDIA
United Way
of Baroda
United Way
of Mumbai

THAILAND
National Council
on Social Welfare
of Thailand

SINGAPORE
National Council
of Social Service

INDONESIA
Yayasan Mitra
Mandiri

PHILIPPINES
United Way
Philippines

AUSTRALIA
United Way
Australia

**NEW
ZEALAND**
United Way
of Greater
Auckland

International Operations

> "We do not provide charity by parachute drop. We are on the ground, helping to build and rebuild communities."
>
> **Mr. Patel and Mr. Beggan, United Way International**

In the 1960s and 1970s, the world was in a rapid state of change. Technology made it easier to access information about people living in other countries. Television news programs showed what was happening around the world on a daily basis. This changed the way people perceived charities and fund-raising.

United Way of America had helped people in need and crisis in the United States for many years.

In 1974, the organization decided to expand to help people in other countries. The UWA was used as a model to create similar organizations all over the world. There are now forty-one countries with one or more United Way chapters in operation.

The United Way International is based in Virginia. It introduced the world to a method of fund-raising through partnerships and shared resources. Its aim is to make the world a better place to live in, here in the United States as well as on the other side of the world.

In 1998, the Beijing chapter of the United Way raised more than $72 million dollars in three days. The money helped those affected by flooding along the Yangtze River in China. The floods destroyed nearly 8 million homes.

United Way

Honors

SHI CHENXUAN

Representing China Charity Federation Beijing, China

Sacramento City Hall January 9, 2001

CASE STUDY
International Cooperation

United Way organizations around the world often work together to raise funds. In Korea, United Way is called Community Chest. In 2000, Community Chest joined forces with the YWCA in Flushing, New York to raise money for children's services. The two organizations hosted a fund-raising lunch for the First Lady of Korea, Mrs. Lee Hee-ho. United Way members wanted to recognize her dedication to the well-being of children. In one day, the event raised $100,000. The money was used to help children in Harlem and Flushing, New York, as well as children in North Korea and Africa.

In the United States, the donation funded many urban-youth agencies. In the African countries of Kenya, Nigeria, South Africa, and Zimbabwe, the money helped children with HIV/AIDS and orphans whose parents had died of the disease. In North Korea, the funds were split between UNICEF of Korea, Korea Welfare Foundation, and the Eugene Bell Foundation. This joint fund-raising effort shows how United Way organizations can cooperate and help people in need on different continents.

Milestones

The United Way has been working with community-based organizations throughout the United States since the 1880s, and around the world since 1974. By 1948, more than 1,000 communities across the country had established United Way chapters.

The 1920s

Fund-raising methods are being explored in the United States during the 1920s. More and more, fund-raising has a national focus. Communities work together to raise more money than ever before for people in need. Community Chests, the name used by United Way organizations, begin to grow during this decade. In 1919, there are thirty-nine Community Chests in the country. By 1929, that number has risen to 353.

1888

The first United Way campaign is launched in Denver, Colorado.

1913

The first modern Community Chest is established in Cleveland, Ohio.

1918

Twelve leaders of fund-raising organizations form the American Association for Community Organizations (AACO). This organization is created to focus on community planning and to develop better standards for community organizations to follow in social work.

1919

Rochester, New York, adopts the name Community Chest. This term is used in the U.S. until the 1950s.

The 1930s

The United States, along with much of the world, falls on hard economic times. The **Great Depression** makes meeting basic needs, such as food and shelter, a challenge for many people. United Way chapters across the country respond. While money is scarce, United Way campaigns raise millions of dollars to help less fortunate Americans. Donations from companies become very important. Now, corporations are able to deduct a percentage of their contribution at tax time.

1927

During this year, 314 communities raise almost $69 million for people in need.

1931

Community Chests unite to fight hunger and poverty caused by the Great Depression, which lasts from 1929 to the early 1940s. More than $100 million is raised in 1931, thanks in part to the first televised appeal for donations. This telethon is aired on CBS on October 10.

1935

With encouragement from the United Way, the federal government changes tax laws to encourage businesses to make donations. Corporations can deduct up to 5 percent of their incomes for charity.

1944

Nearly 800 United Way organizations raise $222 million for war-related programs.

The 1940s

World War II erupts. In 1942, United Way creates the National War Fund to collect money for war-related charitable programs. Almost $167 million is raised during this campaign alone, which is a 53 percent increase over earlier campaigns. Henry Ford II launches the United Health and Welfare Fund in 1947.

Henry Ford II

The 1960s

Health and welfare become major concerns in the U.S. Organizations and agencies are established to fight the new war on poverty. The decade sees a rise in donations and volunteers. In 1967, the United Way raises more than $700 million. In 1967 alone, the United Way welcomes a total of 31,300 agencies to its membership. These agencies help 27.5 million families, as 8.5 million people give their time as volunteers. About 32.8 million people donate to the United Way.

1972

A national group, the National Academy for Voluntarism (NAV) is created. It offers education to United Way professionals and volunteers to help run the organization.

1973

UWA releases Standards of Excellence for United Way Organizations. The guidelines are still recognized standards in the United States. They were updated in 1988.

1974

United Ways in Canada and the U.S. raise more than $1 billion during this year's campaigns. It is the first time that an organization has raised this much money in one year.

1949

Detroit becomes the first city to adopt the name United Fund rather than Community Chest.

1957

The Uniform Federal Fund-Raising Program is introduced, allowing campaigners to ask federal employees for donation pledges.

1963

Los Angeles, California, is the first chapter to formally change its name to United Way. More than thirty Community Chests and United Funds in California unite to form United Way Inc.

1970

The national association renames itself and becomes the United Way of America. Member organizations are encouraged to take on the name "United Way" as well. In 1971, the United Way of America headquarters moves from New York City to Alexandria, Virginia.

1974

The United Way International is established. It helps countries around the world create their own organizations following the successful United Way model.

1976

National volunteers, United Way volunteers, and labor leaders develop the Program for the Future. It offers a plan for the next ten years and provides ways to meet national goals using volunteer power. This program leads to fund-raising growth the following year, when more than $100 million is raised for the first time.

1981

United Ways in the United States raise $1.68 billion in 1981. This is more than a 10 percent increase from 1980.

1982

UWA opens America's National Service and Training Center to train United Way employees and volunteers.

1987

The United Way celebrates its 100th birthday. In recognition of the

The 1970s

In the 1970s, the United Way adopts a new name and continues to provide a high level of service. A national body, the United Way of America, is introduced. During the 1970s, there are many changes to federal laws regarding charities. These changes are intended to help organized fund-raisers, such as the United Way, be more successful. However, some legislation fails. In 1972, the Revenue Sharing Bill is given $30.2 billion over five years. The United Way hopes that state and local governments will use the money to ease important social problems. This does not happen. In spite of this, the United Way continues to raise money for worthy causes, exceeding fund-raising records during the decade.

organization and its volunteers, the U.S. Postal Service produces a special postage stamp. In Washington, DC, more than 3,000 people participate in the Centennial Volunteer Leaders Conference. It is the largest United Way conference ever to be held.

1988

Project Blueprint is established by the UWA with a grant from the W. K. Kellogg Foundation. Eighteen communities receive funds to encourage minority volunteerism and to support minority organizations.

1989

United Ways in Chicago, Houston, Rochester, Pontiac, and York are given $100,000 from the United Way of America's Housing Initiative program. This program, funded by the Ford Foundation, manages housing for lower-income families.

1993

UWA commits to a twenty-year national initiative called Mobilization for America's Children. It provides children with the strategies they need to succeed.

1994

United Way of America is named the charity of choice by Financial World magazine.

1995

The Atlanta Committee for the Olympic Games choose UWA and the United Way system to organize volunteers and community support for the torch relay.

1999

The United Way receives two major donations. The Bank of America Foundation gives $50 million over five years to branches in twenty-two states. Bill Gates, founder of Microsoft, donates $10.5 million to the United Way.

2002

Brian A. Gallagher is appointed president and chief executive officer of United Way of America.

The 1980s

Americans become more aware of the need to protect the environment during the 1980s. The roles for women and minority groups also change. As a result, many new organizations are added to the United Way family. These focus on women's issues, the environment, social action, and human rights. The UWA and its National Service and Training Center are available to offer advice to these new organizations. This decade also marks the 100th birthday of the United Way.

1990

The United Way National Committee on Education and Literacy aims to stamp out adult **illiteracy** with $700,000 in grants from the United Parcel Service. Literacy programs in Kentucky, Indiana, Maryland, Minnesota, North Carolina, and Ohio receive a much-needed boost.

1990

United Way partners team up to help victims of the California earthquake in 1989. The NFL donates $1.25 million and Sony Corporation of America gives $1 million to fund the relief efforts. Americans are also generous. For the first time, Americans donate more than $3 billion to United Way campaigns.

1991

UWA works closely with the American military, the American Red Cross, and other organizations to help those in need after war erupts in the Persian Gulf. The Operations Center at the UWA receives about 1,000 phone inquiries each week during the war.

Current Initiatives

September 11, 2001, Relief Effort

September 11, 2001, will live on in the minds of Americans forever. Immediately following the **terrorist** attacks, the United Way created the September 11th Fund to raise money for the response teams at Ground Zero and the Pentagon. The fund raised more than $425 million in the six months following the disaster. The money raised helped 3,248 people who were badly injured or had lost loved ones, 32,500 people who lost their jobs because of the attacks, and 3,000 people who lost their homes.

> "This is one of those few days in life that one can actually say will change everything."
>
> **EU External Relations Commissioner Chris Patten**

Another $450 million was donated by people around the world. This money was used to provide services to those devastated by the attacks. Grief counselors were provided for both victims and rescue workers. Thousands of people were given support and help finding new jobs after the collapse of the Twin Towers. In addition, United Way chapters helped hundreds of other organizations and businesses rebuild the community.

The United Way knows that it will take time to address all of the needs of the affected communities. The September 11th Fund and many other organizations pledged to continue supporting these communities over the years.

Quick Fact

On September 21, 2001, celebrities helped raise $116 million towards the September 11th Fund during the telethon, America: A Tribute to Heroes. More than thirty television networks and television stations broadcast the program without commercials and without a fee. Stars, including Tom Hanks, Julia Roberts, and Brad Pitt, gave speeches, answered telephones, and recorded pledges.

CASE STUDY
Operation Helping Hands

The attacks on September 11, 2001, devastated communities, but they also brought communities together. At first, many people who lived a long way from the attack sites did not know how to help. People in South Florida were soon shown what they could do to help the relief efforts. The United Way of Miami–Dade found willing partners in The Herald, El Nuevo Herald, NBC, Telemundo Channel 51, and Hispanic Broadcasting Corporation to resume Operation Helping Hands (OHH). This initiative was first established in 1998 to help victims of hurricanes Mitch and George. OHH is reactivated in times of serious need, such as September 11. OHH worked together with the September 11th Fund to raise money for organizations and agencies aiding those affected by the attacks.

As early as September 12, 2001, the operation's partners began collecting corporate contributions. Several banks opened their doors and established donation sites. They also made donations to the September 11th Fund. Bank United gave $10,000 directly to OHH, and Ocean Bank contributed $25,000. Ocean Bank employees also held bake sales and sold American flag pins to raise money for OHH. Companies around Florida did all they could to support the campaign. A Miami real estate company raised $12,000 for OHH. It matched each dollar contributed by its employees and associates. Club Space in Miami put on a fund-raiser with a pizza restaurant. Together they raised $23,500 for OHH and the New York City police and fire departments. The United Way of Miami–Dade is just one example of the strength and compassion shown after September 11th.

NFL Partnership

Since 1973, the United Way of America has teamed up with the National Football League (NFL) to promote the United Way's initiatives. Both organizations thought that a partnership would boost United Way programs and create stronger bonds between football players and their communities. The NFL uses its television airtime during game telecasts to let viewers know about the good works of the United Way. This partnership has strengthened through the years. Today, it is responsible for the Thanksgiving Day Halftime Show, Hometown Huddle, and public service announcements.

Public service announcements have become a well-known outcome of the partnership. In these television announcements, football players talk about supporting their communities through United Way programs. Approximately 113 million people see these announcements every week during the football season. This is a great opportunity for the United Way to get its message to a large audience. The NFL partnership has increased public awareness of the United Way. The NFL-United Way partnership is as strong as ever, with football heroes donating their time and the league offering airtime to help make a difference in the community.

> "While the names and faces have changed over the years, one thing remains constant—our desire to help improve the lives of people in the communities we serve."
>
> **Paul Tagliabue, NFL Commissioner**

The NFL and UWA partnership is the longest-running charitable partnership of its kind in the United States.

Quick Fact

During the Super Bowl, a United Way and NFL commercial is seen by more than 130 million people in the United States and by another 800 million around the world.

CASE STUDY
Hometown Huddle

NFL players speak to children in their communities about staying in school, helping the elderly, and providing housing for those who cannot afford it. Each year, the NFL and the United Way host Hometown Huddle, a day of community service across the country. Members of each NFL team participate in a project that makes their communities safer and stronger. Each year, more than 300 team representatives and players, along with their families, take part in thirty-one Hometown Huddles. Many projects were tackled in 2001.

- The Dallas Cowboys hosted a junior football training camp at the team's complex. It was offered to children receiving assistance from United Way agencies.
- The Green Bay Packers participated in a neighborhood festival. Two hundred children gathered to play games and take part in activities with the players. The team also provided children with school supplies.
- The Washington Redskins established a Redskins/United Way Game Room at the local Boys & Girls Club.
- The San Francisco 49ers helped clean playgrounds, paint planter boxes, and plant flowers.

Hometown Huddles allow sports celebrities to help their communities through volunteering. These events remind people of the difference they can make by giving some time to their communities.

Take Action!

Become an active and responsible citizen by taking action in your community. Participating in local projects can have far-reaching results. You can do service projects no matter where you live. In fact, young people are helping out every day. Some help support overseas projects. Others volunteer for projects in their home communities. Here are some suggestions:

There are many ways that you can become involved in United Way organizations. Most communities in the United States have a United Way chapter. This chapter will have projects and campaigns underway to benefit your community. No matter how large or small the organization or community, your help can make a difference. Find out about the initiatives your United Way is participating in to see how you can help. Everyone, from the very young to the very old, can volunteer his or her time. You could help give a playground a coat of paint or clean up a park. It does not take much to make a difference in your community.

Collecting donations is another way to support the United Way. People may wonder if their small contribution can make a difference. In fact, every penny collected helps people in need and improves lives. At your school, you can ask your teacher to help plan a penny drive for your class or school. Students can donate their spare change. You would be amazed at how quickly the nickels and dimes add up.

Where to Write

International	United States	Canada
United Way International 701 North Fairfax St. Alexandria, VA 22314 United States	**United Way of America** 701 North Fairfax Street Alexandria, VA 22314	**United Way of Canada** Centraide Canada Suite 404, 56 Sparks St. Ottawa, ON K1P 5A9
United Way and United Trusts Post Office Box 14 8 Nelson Road Liverpool L69 7AA UK		
United Way of Australia GPO Box 4083 Sydney NSW 2001 Australia		

In the Classroom

Make Your Own Brochure

Organizations such as the United Way use brochures to inform the public about their activities. To make your own United Way brochure, you will need:
- paper
- ruler
- pencil
- color pens or markers

1. Using your ruler as a guide, fold a piece of paper into three equal parts. Your brochure should now have a cover page, a back page, and inside pages.
2. Using your color markers, design a cover page for your brochure. Make sure you include a title.
3. Divide the inside pages into sections. Use the following questions as a guide.
   - What is the organization?
   - How did it get started?
   - Who started it?
   - Who does it help?
4. Summarize in point form the key ideas for each topic. Add photographs or illustrations.
5. On the back page, write down the address and contact information for the United Way.
6. Photocopy your brochure and give copies to your friends, family, and classmates.

Send a Letter to Your Congressperson

To express concern about a particular issue, you can write a letter to your member of congress. This can be an effective way to make the government aware of issues that need its attention. To write a letter, all you need is a pen and paper or a computer.

1. Find out the name and address of your congressperson by contacting your local librarian. You can also search the Internet.
2. Write your name, address, and phone number at the top of the letter.
3. When addressing your letter, use the congressperson's official title.
4. Outline your concerns in the body of the letter. Share any personal experiences you may have that relate to your concerns. Use information found in this book to strengthen your concerns.
5. Request a reply to your letter. This ensures that your letter has been read.
6. Ask your friends and family to write their own letters.

Further Reading

Duper, Linda Leeb. *160 Ways to Help the World: Community Service Projects for Young People*. New York: Facts on File, 1996.

Erlbach, Arlene. *The Kid's Volunteering Book*. Minneapolis, MN: Lerner Publishing Company, 1998.

Isler, Claudia. *Volunteering to Help in Your Neighborhood*. New York: Children's Press, 2000.

Lewis, Barbara A. *Kids With Courage: True Stories About Young People Making a Difference*. Minneapolis, MN: Free Spirit Publishing, 1992.

Web Sites

ProPoor
www.propoor.com
At the ProPoor Web site, visitors can read about the success stories of volunteer and fund-raising work in South Asia. Another section highlights the stories of those still in need of assistance.

United Way International
www.uwint.org
The United Way International Web site links United Way organizations from all over the world. Visitors can link to various international United Ways or learn about current initiatives in the global community.

United Way of America
national.unitedway.org
The United Way of America Web site provides visitors with the latest news and information on the organization. Visitors can find their local United Way by entering their zip code in the My United Way section.

Glossary

blood transfusions: injections of blood to replace blood that has been lost or not produced

collaborating: working with another person or group in order to achieve something

grants: sums of money given by the government or some other organization to fund a program

Great Depression: an economic collapse in the 1930s

illiteracy: inability to read or write

initiative: programs that are part of a larger project

legislation: a law or laws passed by an official body, usually the government

salvage: rescue from wreckage

terrorist: a person who commits violent activities for political reasons

welfare: health and well-being

Index